ART
+
COFFEE

featuring
TRISTAN EATON
RICARDO CAVOLO
JESSIE + KATEY
LAOLU

photography by
MORGAN IONE YEAGER

text by
FIORELLA VALDESOLO

FOREWORD

At Starbucks, artistry, storytelling, and an irrational passion for coffee are at the heart of everything we do. Whether it's a farmer attentively growing coffee cherries, our master roasters and blenders coaxing the ideal flavors from every bean, or the barista thoughtfully crafting your favorite beverage, we aim to elevate and celebrate the humble ritual of your morning cup of coffee every day.

In that spirit, we invited several influential artists from outside the walls of Starbucks to join us in an exploration of coffee's journey from farm to cup. We asked each artist to immerse in an element of coffee creation and interpret their experiences through their artwork and storytelling. The result was a reimagining of our coffee stories through a limited-edition series of packaging honoring our iconic coffees.

We brought **Tristan Eaton** to Sumatra to experience coffee at its origin. **Ricardo Cavolo** came to Seattle to witness the art and science of roasting alongside our master roasters. **Jessie + Katey** also visited us in Seattle to learn the delicate intricacies of coffee blending from our expert coffee blenders. And **Laolu Senbanjo** spent time in New York City, visiting our partners (employees) in the stores to immerse himself in the sense of connection and humanity that comes to life around coffee.

This book tells the deeper tale of the artists' experiences with us, and the evolution of their art from inspiration to finished piece, finding the parallels between an original work of art and an amazing cup of coffee. From the seedling of an idea to the nurturing of flavor and concept, to humanity, personal connection, and community, we trace the integral elements of creation that are required and cherished in art and coffee alike.

Starbucks has a vast history and a rich tapestry of many stories to be told and this is but a moment in time, a portrait of the coffee origin, blending, roasting, and community that happens every single day across the globe.

We have always believed in the power of coffee, art, and story to bring people together. And we hope that this book and these artists, in celebration of our coffees, will contribute meaningfully to this pursuit.

—MARC-KWESI FARRELL
VP, GLOBAL BEVERAGE AND RETAIL INNOVATION
ON BEHALF OF THE STARBUCKS COFFEE TEAM

01

ORIGIN

SUMATRA

○

TRISTAN EATON

COFFEE'S BEAUTIFUL BEGINNING

Long before a drop of coffee makes it into your cup, it begins with a seed being planted by a farmer somewhere in the world. Somewhere remarkable: coffee grows in the world's most beautiful places, like the highlands of Guatemala's Fraijanes Plateau, or deep in Rwanda's Rift Valley, or in dense jungle thickets in Indonesia. To get a sense of this long, intricate journey, we traced it back to a seedling's beginnings in one of coffee's many origins: Sumatra, the second-largest island among Indonesia's archipelago. Sumatra's landscape is a wildly diverse topography of green mountain slopes, volcanoes, immaculate beaches, jungles, crater lakes, plus a storybook assortment of animal life—it's the only place on earth where tigers, orangutans, elephants, and rhinos live together. It's also the birthplace of the some of the world's most distinctive coffee: full-bodied, smooth, and with a heady intensity. It's coffee that, in the Starbucks story, holds a special lore.

In Sumatra, the only
consistent thing is
its wildness. In no
other origin would
these conditions be
viable for creating
delicious coffee.

—ANDRES BERRON

Tristan Eaton, a Los Angeles–based street artist known for his large-scale freehand murals, traveled to Sumatra to capture the spirit of the singular coffee and the island from which it emanates. While you can spot Eaton's work gracing city walls around the globe, he knew little of Sumatra. "I had to go there to really understand the place and the coffee so the visuals I created didn't just become a cool piece of art, but have a back story too," he says. "It's very remote: it took me twenty-seven hours to get to Sumatra, and that alone gave me an appreciation for how far this coffee travels around the world." While in Sumatra, Eaton visited different locations that impact coffee along its journey from soil to cup with two Starbucks partners who are very knowledgeable about coffees from the region: Andres Berron, a green coffee trader, and Dr. Surip Mawardi.

I'm a regular coffee drinker, but before visiting Sumatra, how the coffee got to my cup was a mystery to me.

—TRISTAN EATON

Q+A

Dr. Surip Mawardi
*Sumatra Country
Manager and Agronomist*

HOW DID YOU FIRST START WORKING AT STARBUCKS?

I was a coffee breeder at the Indonesian Coffee and Cocoa Research Institute (ICCRI) for thirty-four years until I retired in November of 2014. When I was still working at ICCRI, I was invited by Starbucks to support their annual Origin Experience trip to Sumatra, which is attended by company partners from Asia and the Pacific region in order to provide information about coffee growing in Indonesia. I was eventually asked by Starbucks to establish a Farmer Support Center (FSC) located in Sumatra in 2015. My role at the FSC is as a country manager and a lead coffee agronomist.

WHAT DOES YOUR WORK AS A COFFEE AGRONOMIST ENTAIL?

I train coffee growers in best practices on growing coffee to get the highest yield and optimal quality so they can improve their livelihood. Best practices consist of the use of superior coffee varieties, land preparation, planting systems, shade tree management, soil and water conservation, fertilizer application, pest and disease control, integrated farming, cherry harvesting, and post-harvest processing, all with the goal of sustainable coffee production. The people I'm working with in Indonesia are a lot of smallholding coffee farmers in various remote villages.

WHAT IS SO SPECIAL ABOUT THE COFFEE FROM SUMATRA?

The taste of Sumatran coffee is what makes it so unique. It's characterized mainly by a full-bodied mouthfeel, lower acidity, and complex flavor with a light, earthy note. When it's still a green bean, Sumatra coffee is a beautiful deep blue-green color with the appearance of jade. Sumatra coffee's singular quality comes thanks to both geographic factors and the traditional means local people use to pick and process mature coffee cherries.

HOW HAVE YOU SEEN THE COFFEE INDUSTRY SHIFT SINCE YOU STARTED WORKING FOR STARBUCKS?

Climate change is one of the most important issues impacting coffee production. Coffee production has decreased due to climate change's impact on flowering traits as well as more pest and disease attacks. But the willingness of farmers to apply best practices to grow coffee is getting better. And consumers are becoming more knowledgeable about coffee flavor and quality—and more curious about the back story behind the coffee they're drinking, which is exciting.

WHERE COFFEE COMES FROM

The world's "coffee belt" is made up of the countries nestled between the equatorial band of the Tropics of Cancer and Capricorn. The climate and terrain in these areas—higher elevations that see warmer daytime and cooler nighttime temperatures—are ideal for growing the arabica coffee Starbucks uses. While coffee is one of the most popular beverages globally, drinkers may not realize that the source of what's in their cup comes from inside a fruit. Coffee cherries grow on evergreen shrubs that can live for over one hundred years and reach a height of more than twenty feet. Once the tree flowers, the fruit forms, starting as a little green seed that will, over the course of nine months, grow and ripen until the cherry is ready to be picked.

MEET THE
COFFEE CHERRY

It's the two beans at the core of each coffee cherry that eventually transform, after processing and roasting, into the coffee we recognize. A cross-section of a cherry reveals that those precious beans are surrounded by a protective silver skin; papery, thin white parchment; sticky, honey-like mucilage; a water and sugar-based pulp; and, finally, a thick outer skin. Parts of the cherry that don't make it into the coffee, like the pulp, are often reused as compost for the fields.

THE HARVESTING

Pruning is critical for maintaining the productivity of a coffee tree. The color that signals ripeness isn't the same from one coffee tree to another: most often it will be red, but it can also be yellow or orange. "A critical step to ensure high-quality arabica coffee is to only pick the ripest cherry," says Berron. "And on one coffee tree, cherries ripen at different times so there are usually at least five pickings in a harvest." These discrepancies in ripening mean handpicking remains the optimal way to ensure the best harvest output. (Coffee trees are usually pruned to hover around six feet to make manual retrieval easier.)

THE YIELD

Coffee grown at lower altitudes may have greater yields, but Starbucks only purchases high-altitude coffee because of its depth of flavor. The yearly output of a single tree is equivalent to one pound of coffee beans, so that means most regular coffee drinkers are brewing a plant's annual harvest in the span of a week.

Sumatra is unique due to its position on the equator—at any given time, there may be a flower, a green cherry, and a red cherry all on the same tree.

—ANDRES BERRON

THE PLANT TRANSFORMED

Just as with wine, terroir (the land where its components are grown) has an impact on coffee's flavor. So does how the coffee is processed. Once the coffee cherries come off the plant, there are several methods for turning it into the green coffee that will be exported: dry, washed, or semi-washed, the last being the most popular process in Sumatra.

DRY

The dry or natural process is especially common in regions like Ethiopia where water is scarce. Cherries are dried for days in the sun until they look raisin-like, then hulled and dried again, resulting in a fruit-forward coffee.

WASHED

Specific processes vary from origin to origin, but in general, cherries are washed and put through de-pulping machines to remove the fruit from the bean. Then beans are left to ferment in tanks for a day then dried for up to a week and rested for two months before being hulled (their outer parchment removed). This method, frequently used in Latin America, yields a more acidic flavor.

SEMI-WASHED

This mash-up of the two processes is often associated with Sumatra. The first steps are completed on the same farms where cherries are harvested. Right after picking, cherries are washed and de-pulped using hand-cranked machines. Next, beans are soaked and partially dried on backyard tarps in the sun before being transported (often strapped to the back of mopeds) to a dry mill. There they are dried for a few more days, then hulled and dried again. This partial drying and lack of fermentation give semi-washed coffee big body and earthy, herbal flavors.

Getting to visit the farms and see the faces behind the coffee was such a relief. It's incredible that a dad operating a farm with his family in remote Sumatra can contribute to a giant coffee culture.

—TRISTAN EATON

Not every picked coffee cherry will end up in your cup; the company's unwavering focus on quality starts at the farm and is visible at every step from bean to cup. The type of trees planted are a considered choice to align with the unpredictable climate of an area with no confined rainy or dry seasons. With that unique climate in mind, the typical farm in North Sumatra uses shade trees: the slightly cooler temperatures they provide allow the soil to retain more moisture. That way, in a season with limited rain, there's another mechanism to allow the root system to maintain more water. And the sorting process is equally exacting: after washing, the beans are evaluated at multiple stages of sorting. Sumatra's special terroir, the signature semi-washed process, and the exacting standards from start to finish combine for a coffee of extraordinary flavor. "The coffee is full-bodied and earthy—not a surprise since it comes from this wild and rich landscape," says Eaton. "It's unlike anything else I've ever had."

THINKING BIG AND SMALL

The biggest surprise to Eaton, considering the enormous global footprint of the company, was the small size of some of the farms where the coffee is actually grown: In Sumatra, backyard farms are the norm. "I drink a lot of Starbucks and I never would have thought that the coffee comes from these individual tiny farms," says Eaton of the small family-run operations he visited. "It's incredible that a family operating a farm in remote Sumatra can contribute to a giant coffee culture." That the coffee-farming process in Sumatra, from the planting to the picking, is a distinctly human one is something that, as a figurative artist who often depicts people in his work, Eaton related to. "There are so many visual cues here, from the beauty and innate style of the people to the wild natural environment to the architecture," he shares. "Traveling through the countryside, I amassed a vocabulary of imagery so my piece would tell the story of this coffee to someone far away from here."

When Eaton is visualizing a new piece, anything and everything around him—even what some might dismiss as minutiae—becomes fodder for artistic inspiration. His time in Sumatra was no exception. The jagged geometry of tire tracks from the scrums of mopeds, laden with sacks of coffee strapped to the back (a regular sight zipping along the winding streets of North Sumatra, transporting cherries from wet mill to dry mill to farm) were visually logged and woven into his work. So too were the intricate patterns on the head scarves worn by the women while they work. "There's so much beauty in the elements of everyday life here," Eaton says. Even the utilitarian mechanisms of a common de-pulping machine, a regular presence on the small coffee farms of North Sumatra since it's an essential tool for wet milling, was a source of inspiration. "I'm always looking for little details that might inform my art, like those little teeth on the drum that pull the pulp off," he says. "They would make a nice embossing mark or print pattern in my painting."

Q+A

Tristan Eaton

TELL US ABOUT YOUR OWN RELATIONSHIP WITH COFFEE.

Coffee is a sacred ritual for me! Not only is it how I wake up in the morning, it's also a designated way to regularly break from my work and contemplate. I'm typically a night owl when I paint, and coffee can be an amazing companion for an artist during those lonely nights.

HAD YOU CONSIDERED, BEFORE YOUR TRIP TO SUMATRA, WHERE THE COFFEE YOU WERE DRINKING COMES FROM?

I never knew the details of the process but I was aware of its many origins (Brazilian versus Jamaican coffee, for example) and how much that could affect flavor. But I don't think the average person thinks too much about where his or her coffee comes from or how it's made. It's such an ever-present, ubiquitous part of our lives that many of us take it for granted. Personally, I can never think of coffee the same way after my amazing journey to Sumatra. It was eye-opening and inspirational.

WHAT WERE SOME OF THE MOST SURPRISING DISCOVERIES YOU MADE ON YOUR TRIP TO SUMATRA?

I was very happily surprised to find how handmade the process still is. Starbucks buys their beans from many small farms, many of which are family run and operated. I think it's easy to imagine that a company as large as Starbucks would have the whole system automated in a giant factory somewhere run by coffee robots, but there I was in North Sumatra with veteran coffee-making families on these beautiful small coffee farms.

HOW DO ART AND COFFEE CONNECT FOR YOU?

I can immediately relate to the pursuit of quality. There is trial and error in coffee and in art making. There is a universal appreciation for people who seek quality—failure after failure, trying over and over relentlessly. This is how you reach greatness. Coffee and art both have very tough audiences to please! Both coffee connoisseurs and art collectors are always looking for the real deal, savoring the classics and celebrating the bold new arrivals. And they are both hard to impress!

CAN YOU TELL US ABOUT THE PIECE YOU CREATED WHILE ON THE TRIP AND THE ART FOR THE LIMITED-EDITION COFFEE PACKAGING?

I really wanted to create a window into this colorful, lively, and beautiful region of Indonesia. I wanted to capture it in all its glory so people would have more insight, more context, and hopefully more admiration and respect for how far this coffee has traveled and how many great people worked hard to get it there. It's truly a beautiful journey.

· ·

SUMATRA

Sumatra coffee has been a treasured Starbucks signature since it was first offered in 1972. This distinctive coffee with an unmistakable flavor is a favorite of many partners and customers.

FLAVOR NOTES
Earthy and herbal

GROWING REGION
Asia/Pacific

BODY
Full

ACIDITY
Low

PROCESSING
Semi-washed

FOOD PAIRINGS
Cheese, breakfast sandwiches

BLONDE   MEDIUM   DARK

ROASTING

SEATTLE

○

RICARDO CAVOLO

A SPECIAL KIND OF ALCHEMY

Once green coffee beans arrive stateside from their country of origin, whether Sumatra or Guatemala or Ethiopia, roasting is what transforms them into the aromatic beans we recognize. The roasting process feels a bit like magic: the metamorphosis of vegetal-tasting green coffee seeds into incredibly complex coffee beans. It's a process to which relatively little consumer attention was paid until the late 1960s, when coffee was increasingly being consumed not only as morning fuel but for its unique flavor. There was also little attention paid to the potential artistry of roasting, and how, when properly manipulated, roasting can dramatically shift and elevate a coffee's flavor. That principle— discovering the true essence of each coffee bean and letting it shine—has been a central tenet of the company's mission from the beginning. The radical shift the beans undergo when they arrive at the roaster: that's where the magic happens.

ROASTERY
COFFEE
ONLY IN
ROWS
5 AND 6

Some of Barcelona-based painter Ricardo Cavolo's earliest memories are framed by the scent of coffee. "As a kid, I would steal coffee beans from my grandmother before she ground them and keep them in the pocket of my trousers because I loved the smell so much," he shared. So Cavolo, whose fantastical portraits and murals have been commissioned for everything from sneakers to tarot cards, was thrilled by the invite to travel to Seattle for an immersion in one of coffee's most sensory processes: roasting. "I knew there was lighter and darker coffee but after a few days here I learned there is so much more that differentiates and contributes to coffee's individual personalities," says Cavolo.

Roasting is about creating personalities with coffee, which is similar to how I work with the idea of character in my portraits.

—RICARDO CAVOLO

ROASTING 101

The mountain of green coffee beans that arrive daily at the Starbucks Seattle roasting plant from the far corners of the globe each have their own fundamental flavor characteristics. The process of roasting—the application of intense heat to tip off a chemical reaction that eventually releases the oils that give coffee its signature taste—is designed to pull out the optimal aroma, body, flavor, and acidity, taking into account that each bean has different needs. There is no uniform time and temperature for coffee roasting: every variety requires its own finessing and nurturing to highlight its best qualities. It's an art, a science, and also a balancing act. During his trip to Seattle, Cavolo spent time with several tenured and knowledgeable partners from the Global Coffee Department, including master roasters Brad Anderson, Brian Hayes, and Dave Wickberg.

> Seeing how complex the actual roasting process is made me think more about each cup of coffee that I drink.
>
> —RICARDO CAVOLO

Technology may have helped streamline the process and ensure consistency but, the human element remains a crucial component of the roasting process. At the heart of this stage of coffee's transformation is the master roaster. In a craft that is both unique and highly specialized, those who have earned the title have learned it by doing. And there are only a few of them. At Starbucks, a company that employs over 300,000 people globally, there are only eight master roasters. "It's an approach that never stops—we're always evaluating and reevaluating, constantly learning as circumstances and the environment change," says Dave Wickberg.

Roasting is like a language—you can only memorize so much. In order to become fluent, you have to have experience.

—BRAD ANDERSON

Q + A

Brian Hayes
Starbucks Master Roaster

HOW DID YOU FIRST START WORKING AT STARBUCKS?

I was first hired for seasonal support after moving to Seattle in 1992, then I was a barista for almost three years before joining the coffee department at the company's Kent, Washington, roasting plant. I eventually moved over to the company's headquarters as a master roaster, where I've been for the past fifteen years. Before working at Starbucks I'd never really cared about or thought of coffee other than as something to keep me awake, but then I realized what a cool industry it is.

WHAT IS THE ROLE OF A MASTER ROASTER?

There are a lot of aspects to the job beyond just overseeing the roasting process. We do all the research and development, the test roasting of new and Starbucks Reserve® coffees, the work on new blends and reformulation of recipes when necessary, the creation of educational presentations, and the training of new roasters. The roasting itself is almost like painting: to do it, you build a good foundation of fundamental knowledge and learn the masters and then you figure out what hasn't been done yet and how to make it your own.

WHAT DO YOU LOVE ABOUT YOUR JOB?

I'm someone who tends to get bored very easily so I have a need to keep adding knowledge and learning about new processes and this job allows me to do that. I'm still a student of the craft so I'm always evolving and doing something a little different and that journey of constantly learning really suits my personality. Most learning comes through actually roasting all different types of coffee and using many different types of machines. That really opens your eyes to all the possibilities, and here at Starbucks we have a roasting playground!

WHAT'S UNIQUE ABOUT THE STARBUCKS APPROACH TO ROASTING?

It may not sound like much, but our consistency is what makes us really unique. If you're going to roast hundreds of millions of pounds of coffee a year, you want your specialty to taste the same in every store on the planet. And we make sure it does.

FIRST POP

Talk about a unique growth spurt: coffee doubles in size when it grows from green seed to roasted kernel. But it also loses much of its original weight because the intense roasting drives off moisture. Just like kernels of popcorn, as coffee seeds absorb the intense roasting heat they lose moisture, expand, get bigger, and eventually, at around 380 degrees, make a distinct "pop" sound.

SECOND POP

The next stage of roasting occurs when beans start emitting heat, resulting in a second popping sound. This happens near the end of the roast, but it is crucial for flavor development.

ROAST SPECTRUM

The application of a certain temperature at a certain time is called a roast curve. When Starbucks is developing new coffees, roasters will apply a variety of different roast profiles to reach the bean's individual peak of aroma, acidity, body, and flavor to create an optimal cup for each profile.

Both with art and roasting, you can have all the technology in the world, but it's the human touch that's really essential.

—RICARDO CAVOLO

THE ROAST SPECTRUM

The spectrum of roasts at Starbucks is wide, but its progression isn't necessarily a straight-forward one from light to dark. Take Sumatra: it's classified as a dark roast though technically it spends less time in the roaster than Pike Place® Roast, but because its flavor is more intense, it's considered darker. So, whether a coffee is light or dark is less about appearance and more about taste: lighter-roasted coffees usually have a higher acidity, while darker-roasted coffees have a fuller body and richness. Historically, Starbucks has been best known for its deeper, headier blends like French Roast. Starbucks® Blonde Roast was introduced in 2013 to fill a specific customer demand for a lighter, more easy-drinking blend. And its creation process was, says Hayes, a cool journey of discovery. "We created over eighty iterations before we were able to track down the elusive flavor," he adds.

Roasting is a combination of art and science. Art is what got us here; science is what keeps us here.

—DAVE WICKBERG

AN IDEA
TAKES FLIGHT

Raised by artists, Cavolo has had a paintbrush in hand since he was a kid. His approach, which pulls heavily from the folk tradition of using art as a forum for telling a tale, was a natural fit to conjure roasting's story. For Cavolo, fire, an essential element and catalyst in the roasting process, had to be front and center, and just as important was expressing coffee's varieties using the best tool he had: color. "I wanted to include the full spectrum of different shades of brown to show all the shades that roasting brings out," he explains. Cavolo found a lot of commonality between the age-old processes of painting and coffee roasting. "For both, you need instinct and technique, and to be constantly evolving and adding new ideas to your process," he says. "Just like a visual artist, a master roaster has a vision in mind before starting. Then it's about trying different things to get to that end point. Innovation is all about trial and error."

Q+A

Ricardo Cavolo

Once I understood how fundamental roasting is in the coffee process and to its final result, I decided to do something similar when creating the colors to paint with. I carefully mixed colors until I found the one I was looking for, in the same way that Starbucks experiments with roasting until they reach the flavor and aroma they desire.

CAN YOU DESCRIBE A FEW KEY ELEMENTS OF THE COFFEE
PACKAGING ART?

Above all, I wanted to nod to the nuances of the smells from the roasting process and my chromatic palette offers a clue to the world of coffee aromas. The birds are like drops of coffee flying joyfully onto your palate. I envisioned the master roaster almost like an ancient goddess with vast knowledge. And I also wanted to emphasize the importance of the human touch in the roasting process so I included a hand holding a large coffee bean full of fire, to allude to this idea of managing the fire—of something wild that has to be tamed by the hands of an expert.

HOW IS THE ART FOR THE PACKAGING DIFFERENT THAN
THE SITE-SPECIFIC PIECE YOU CREATED?

There is a strong message and approach that unifies them. In both works, I wanted to emphasize the prism that is the human touch that controls something wild like fire to tame the coffee bean and lead it where it is desired in terms of taste, aroma, and experience of the coffee drinker.

WHAT DO YOU WANT THE PACKAGING ART TO EVOKE FOR
THE CUSTOMER?

Drinking coffee is an experience that can connect us and I want customers when they see my work to be full of joy, strength, and optimism.

VERANDA BLEND®

This coffee, the first blonde roast Starbucks created, took over two years (and eighty recipes) to develop. It was created for customers who prefer a lighter roast and more mellow flavor.

FLAVOR NOTES
Mellow and soft

BODY
Light

PROCESSING
Washed

GROWING REGION
Latin America

ACIDITY
Medium

FOOD PAIRINGS
Chocolate chip cookies, banana nut bread

BLONDE   MEDIUM   DARK

GUATEMALA ANTIGUA

This coffee gets its hallmark flavor from the unique growing conditions in the nutrient-rich Antigua Valley, where the coffee plants grow, surrounded by volcanoes, at an altitude of five thousand feet.

FLAVOR NOTES
Cocoa and subtle spice

BODY
Medium

PROCESSING
Washed

GROWING REGION
Latin America

ACIDITY
Medium

FOOD PAIRINGS
Apple strudel, chocolate croissants

BLONDE   MEDIUM   DARK

CAFFÈ VERONA®

First developed in 1975, Caffè Verona was crafted to pair with a chocolate dessert. Chocolate is still a perfect complement to this long-standing customer and partner favorite.

FLAVOR NOTES
Earthy and herbal

BODY
Full

PROCESSING
Semi-washed

GROWING REGION
Asia/Pacific

ACIDITY
Low

FOOD PAIRINGS
Brownies, salted caramel

BLONDE   MEDIUM   DARK

03

BLENDING

SEATTLE

o

JESSIE + KATEY

A PRACTICE BORN OUT OF DISCOVERY

One of the world's first coffee blends dates all the way back to the eighteenth century. Traders on ocean-bound journeys between Europe and the Asian continent would often stop and pick up coffee beans from the island of Java in Indonesia and the fabled port of Mocha in Yemen. Once they arrived back at home, the Dutch traders blended the two together, discovering that the Indonesian coffee's rich earthiness was perfectly offset by the citrus-laced brightness of the variety from Yemen. And thus was born the iconic (and still frequently re-created by many coffee companies) Mocha Java blend and, more importantly, the merging of different coffee strains to create hybrid brews. That desire holds strong at Starbucks, where blending is at the essence of signatures like Pike Place® Roast. Much like the roasting process, blending is a marriage of artistry and technique, where the creativity and skill of a master blender is integral in crafting a singular cup.

Baltimore-based painting duo Jessie Unterhalter and Katey Truhn are known for their large-scale works that play with geometrical shapes and bright colors and have transformed public spaces everywhere from Hawaii to Washington, D.C., to Russia. "Most of our work is in the public sphere so before we approach a new artwork we always consider how people will be experiencing the final piece," the pair says. "This is very true of the coffee blender as well. Their aim is the same: to make a blend that people will enjoy." Starbucks invited the pair to their Seattle headquarters to see just what goes into identifying flavor profiles and creating a new blend of coffee.

We knew a bit about the coffee-harvesting process having once visited farms in Central America, but had no idea what cupping or blending was, or how much thought and creativity went into making a cup of coffee.

—JESSIE UNTERHALTER

BUILDING
A RECIPE

Coffee and food have a lot in common. Much like with cooking, often you don't need a lot of ingredients—just a few high-quality ones—to create something complex and delicious. And building a coffee's profile is similar to building a recipe: At Starbucks, a team of three master blenders consider which ingredients or coffee origins will help them achieve the desired taste profile. "Our recipes always have three components: acidity, body, and complexity, and each one should bring something to the blend," says master blender Anthony Carroll. "It's always about figuring out how to align these elements to make a clean and balanced cup."

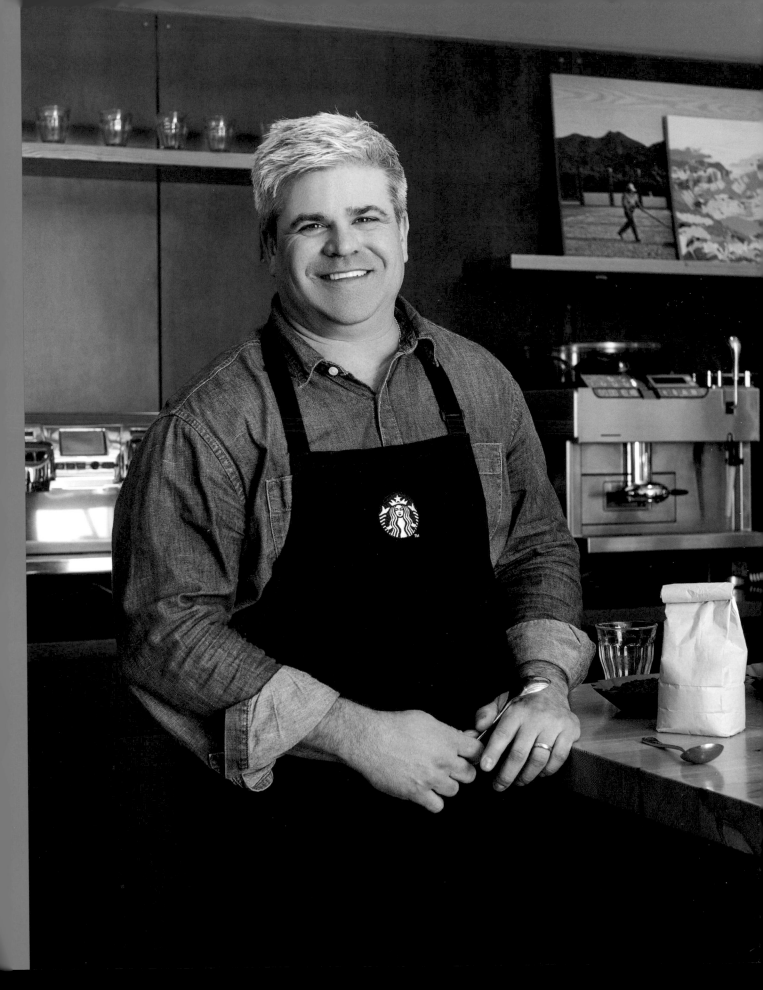

Q+A

Anthony Carroll
Master Blender

HOW DID YOU FIRST START WORKING AT STARBUCKS?

I moved to Seattle from the mountains of Colorado in 1995 and started working as a barista. Over the course of the next ten years I cycled through a bunch of different jobs at the company, from financial analyst to product innovation to customer service. I became a green-coffee quality specialist and worked in marketing before finally taking over the blend development process.

WHAT DOES WORKING IN BLEND DEVELOPMENT ENTAIL?

For me, it's like making food. For example, you have a red sauce at your favorite Italian restaurant that you want to re-create at home so you start thinking of all the ingredients you might need to get you to that final flavor profile. And that's the way I've always thought about and taught blending: consider what you want the final result to be, then deconstruct it and rebuild it again.

WHEN IT COMES TO COFFEE FLAVOR, WOULD YOU SAY STARBUCKS HAS A SPECIFIC CREDO?

Blending is a part of the Starbucks DNA. It's important that we create flavor profiles that are very unique and can only be produced by us. Another part of the Starbucks signature is the dark roast, the blend we're known for, and using only the highest-quality coffee beans. We've expanded the flavor experience but it's rooted in that history.

"There are many variables and possible outcomes with coffee blending so it's a lot like making art in that way," says Unterhalter. "You have a vision for something and mix all the components together until you get your desired result." The "paints" you'll find in a Starbucks blender's palette are coffees from various origins separated by the purpose they will serve: acidity, body, and complexity. Multiple origins show up in each basket: in acidity, you might find coffee from Costa Rica and Guatemala; in body, Brazil, Nicaragua, and Honduras; and in complexity, Colombia and Ethiopia. "Ultimately, we are trying to paint a picture by mixing these origins together," says Carroll.

Blending has no boundaries. At Starbucks, if we can dream it, we can create it.

—MARY MAYORQUIN

THE BALANCING ACT

Creating an original blend is a collaborative effort between the blending and roasting teams that can take about three months. The blending team starts their process by wet blending: mixing spoonfuls of brewed coffee from various origins until they figure out the most flavorful ratio. Once they've landed on the formula, it's time to dry blend: combining the green coffee beans and roasting them together, then tasting them again to make sure the flavor is where they want it to be. If blenders need more acidity they can have the master roaster tweak the formula of the dry blend, adjusting the bean percentages. And when it comes to creating signature blends, order matters. In a pre-roast blend, green coffee is blended first, then roasted. A post-roast blend is reserved for coffees whose flavors, if you roasted them together, would get lost in the mix. So, to ensure that each is given a chance to shine, they are roasted separately to their individual peaks then blended together afterwards.

"Cupping" is the industry term for the process of evaluating coffee before it's roasted. First, an immersion brew of a small quantity of coffee beans is made; in the concentrated cup the flavors are exaggerated so blenders can taste the good, the bad, and the ugly. First, you smell, or as insiders call it, "break the crust," using a spoon to dip in and release a coffee's aroma. "It gives you the first indication of what the coffee is going to taste like," says Carroll. Next, you slurp. That's right, slurping is encouraged because it aspirates the coffee and gives you the full impact of the flavor in your mouth.

TASTING CHECKLIST

There are four factors to keep in mind when evaluating any coffee: aroma, acidity, body, and flavor. Here's how to toot your palate.

AROMA

Smelling spices and herbs can be a great way to fine-tune your nose. Compare fresh sage versus parsley, or ground cinnamon versus cumin and try to describe what the scent reminds you of. Is it pungent? Nutty? More floral or perhaps earthy?

ACIDITY

Some coffees are described as smooth, while others have an inherent brightness; this is determined by acidity, which is the tanginess or tartness. Try sipping orange juice then water and make a note of how each feels different on your tongue.

BODY

A coffee's body or mouthfeel is exactly what it sounds like: how heavy it feels when you take a sip. To experience the sensation of different weights, drink nonfat milk first, then whole.

FLAVOR

The more adventurous of an eater you are, the broader your individual palate will be. The cheese aisle happens to be a great place to develop a flavor vocabulary: try to taste and describe the differences between cheddar, mozzarella, camembert, and feta.

FLAVOR
BY ORIGIN

"You quickly realize after just one round of tasting how the flavor of coffee from different regions is completely unique," says Truhn. Latin American coffees are known for their refreshing acidity and their cocoa and nutty flavors; African coffees are often lush and floral with a hint of citrus and spice; and coffees from the Asia/Pacific region tend to be rich and syrupy with an herbaceous earthiness. As coffee culture has evolved, customers have become more interested than ever in origin. "That interest is exciting for us because if people understand the flavors of different origins it also gives them a newfound appreciation for what's in their blend as well," says Mary Mayorquin, coffee development manager.

THINKING IN LAYERS

Though Unterhalter and Truhn make art as individuals as well, it's as a team that they've discovered an inspiring synergy that has translated into the dynamic abstractions for which they've become known. "Working as a duo is so cool because we get to create something that's more than ourselves—something that we couldn't do on our own," explains Truhn. "And the result has an element of surprise every time," adds Unterhalter. The pair discovered overlaps with this artistic MO, and that of the cupping and blending teams. "We're very process-based artists and our work is usually multi-stepped and fairly laborious so we really identified with them," says Truhn. For their on-site mural they approached it, as blenders do, in layers. "They taste all these coffees and consider how to make them cohesive, and we were thinking in the same way about how our layers of colors and shapes would come together," says Truhn. In the final work, winding strands of coffee beans thread all the colorful panels together.

Q+A

Jessie ǀ Katey

HOW WOULD YOU DESCRIBE YOUR ARTISTIC APPROACH?

Our approach is 100 percent collaborative. We try to stand in a space before we begin working because the context and the architecture influence our design. Then we re-create the space on paper and hit the drawing board. We often work in layers. The first layer is the larger shapes that tie the overall space together, and the second layer is the line work and patterns that then tie the larger shapes together. Then we pass the drawing back and forth between adding different options.

WHAT INSPIRED THE ART YOU CREATED FOR THE STARBUCKS COFFEE PACKAGING?

The color palette is always the most important element for us! It's the first thing people see and it really sets the mood. In our design for the limited-edition Pike Place® Roast packaging, the colors are warm and bright and bold, and directly inspired by our walk through the market. When paired with coffee plant imagery, the palette feels almost tropical, our shout-out to the early stages of the coffee process and the climate in which it's grown. Look closely at the design and you'll notice some references to the Pike Place store and its surrounding environment: there are brick and water patterns as well as a repetition of dahlias (an icon of the flower stalls at the market) tied together by curvy, integrated line work.

HOW IS THE ART FOR THE PACKAGING DIFFERENT THAN THE SITE-SPECIFIC PIECE YOU CREATED?

The two projects were completely different: for the mural, we were engaging the space with a more abstract approach and trying to specifically reference the blending workshops by having our shapes and color overlap. The design for the packaging was very specific to Pike Place; there's a lot of history and pride in the Pike Place Roast and we wanted to capture that with the imagery and color. We want devoted Starbucks customers to feel jazzed when they see it!

HOW DID YOU APPROACH THE CHALLENGE OF SCALING DOWN AND/OR REIMAGINING YOUR ART FOR THE PACKAGING?

We actually started by drawing on a cardboard coffee tube. The image was never going to be seen all at once on a wall or flat canvas, so we wanted to better understand how to tackle the composition. It was unlike any other surface we had ever painted on! We made about ten different designs before we chose one to really focus on. It was a challenge to make all the imagery tie together in such a small area while keeping the composition dynamic and interesting.

'71

PIKE PL.

1912 PIKE PI.

· ·

PIKE PLACE® ROAST

Developed in 2008, this coffee was designed to be both harmonious in flavor and versatile enough to be the Starbucks signature everyday blend. This special recipe of Latin American coffees is carefully blended and roasted in a unique way so that no single flavor dominates or disappears.

FLAVOR NOTES
Smooth and balanced

GROWING REGION
Latin America

BODY
Medium

ACIDITY
Medium

PROCESSING
Washed

FOOD PAIRINGS
Coffee cake, egg-and-cheese breakfast sandwiches

BLONDE   MEDIUM   DARK

04

CONNECTION

IN THE STORE

o

LAOLU

With coffee, it's about nature *and* nurture. The first steps of its creation story—how the coffee plant is cared for and cultivated as a seedling—are no more important than the final step of connecting over a cup of coffee. Starbucks refers to this critical chapter in coffee's life cycle as "the last ten feet," so named for the distance between the barista preparing the coffee and the customer awaiting it. But it didn't start that way: at the shoebox-sized shop that opened in Pike Place Market in 1971, there wasn't a coffee machine in sight. Because the routine for most people at the time was to brew at home, the retail shop sold only whole-bean roasted coffee, plus tea and spices. But when Howard Schultz, who joined Starbucks in the early 1980s, took a trip to Italy and experienced their café culture firsthand, he became intent on importing the idea. A few years later in 1984, Starbucks sold their first latte.

Coffee is a beverage of community. It brings people together.

—SANDY ROBERTS

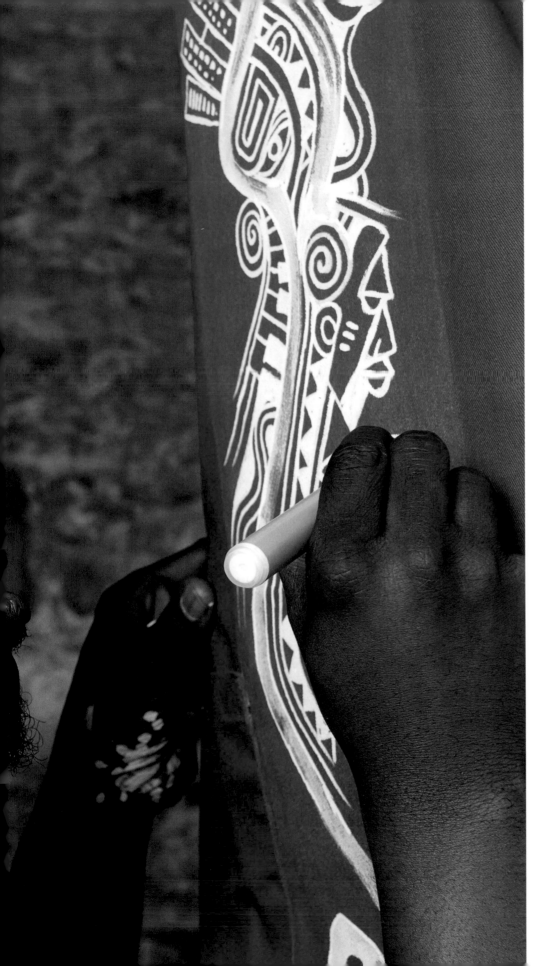

The vivid, wildly
intricate visions drawn
by the Nigeria-born,
Brooklyn-based,
human-rights-lawyer-
turned-performance-
and-visual artist known
simply as Laolu, have
graced leather jackets, bass
guitars, high-tops—even
faces of people. He's
passionate about his native
Yoruba culture, which has
had a deep influence on
his art. "As an artist, you
can be given the tools to
create great work, but if
you don't have the passion,
those tools are useless,
and the same is true with
coffee," he explains. "It
takes time and dedication
to craft and perfect any
art form. Just because you
have an espresso machine
doesn't make you a barista."
Something Laolu learned
when Starbucks invited
him to join baristas at some
of their most popular New
York locations.

The customer connection has always been at the heart of the Starbucks experience. It's amazing what can happen in a store interaction.

—SANDY ROBERTS

Barista craft is at the heart of every cup of coffee served at all Starbucks locations. It is the Starbucks partners wearing the green apron who make the difference in each customer experience. To learn what it means to be a barista at Starbucks, Laolu visited stores in New York and spent time learning from a group of talented partners and other coffee education leaders including Sandy Roberts, director of coffee leadership, and Sandor Petiet, an eleven-year partner and regional coffee ambassador in New York. Laolu agrees that the difference is perceptible: "If a barista doesn't care about what they're doing you can taste that in your drink."

Q+A

Davina Perez
Shift Supervisor

What initially drew me to Starbucks was being a regular at a great location by my school. I came in every day, and everyone who worked there knew what I was getting and would ask me about my classes and what's new in life. Then I began hearing them call each other "partners" and that just sounded so special to me. I thought, "Wow, how can I be a part of this? Where do I sign up?" I am now a two-year partner, thankful to have excelled in becoming both a coffee master and shift supervisor. But my role has changed in greater ways than titles: I started working for Starbucks at a very low point in my life, so when I joined an environment filled with growth, I automatically felt like my role in life changed. I felt more purposeful. I realized I was not only a barista making a latte, but a barista with the power to completely change someone's day and make a connection that was meaningful.

STARBUCKS CALLS THE FINAL STRETCH OF COFFEE'S JOURNEY FROM CROP TO CUP "THE LAST TEN FEET"; WHAT DOES THAT PHRASE MEAN TO YOU? AND WHAT IS ITS SIGNIFICANCE IN COFFEE'S JOURNEY?

The last ten feet are extremely important to me. It's the way we bring the journey of coffee to our stores and customers. It's making the coffee farmers proud and teaching our customers about our different beans and roasts. It's helping that customer who comes in for a tall coffee find their favorite coffee region—do you like Latin American, African, or Asia/Pacific coffees? It's teaching them the notes of each coffee region and helping them find their favorite way to brew and showing them the difference. I love owning the last ten feet at my store.

HOW IMPORTANT IS THE CUSTOMER CONNECTION TO THE STARBUCKS EXPERIENCE? AND HOW CAN THAT INTERACTION RESULT IN A BETTER CUP OF COFFEE?

Customer connection is essential to the Starbucks experience. It's what's gotten us where we are now. If there is no human connection behind each drink, it becomes more transactional, and that's not what we're about. A simple, "Hey, Susan, your latte is coming right up. How's your day going today?" can really impact someone's life. Each beverage served with no interaction is one connection that's missed. Customer connection is what has kept me here and what has always drawn me to this company.

WHAT ARE YOUR FAVORITE DRINKS AND COFFEE ART TO MAKE?

My favorite drinks to make are flat whites! I love mastering the dot every time. My favorite art to make is the rosetta! I make really cute ones.

Starbucks® Espresso Roast was developed in 1975, and is still the signature espresso at the core of many beverages served today. The optimal shot of espresso is aromatic, rich, and bold with three levels of flavor. "The crema is the nice, golden brown layer on top, then there's the body of the espresso in the middle, and the darkest most intense notes at the heart," explains Petiet. He adds that baristas taste shots throughout the day to ensure flavor integrity. "Our Espresso Roast paints the tongue with a sweetness in the front, a hint of sour at the sides, and a richness in the back."

Espresso is the heart of our barista's craft. It's the foundation.

—SANDY ROBERTS

The Starbucks Mission—to
inspire and nurture
the human spirit, one
person, one cup, and one
neighborhood at a time—
underscores the company's
unwavering commitment
to supporting communities
around their coffee shops.
Baristas pride themselves
on knowing the names
and drink orders of their
regulars. "Each of our stores
is a community. I was a
customer before I was on the
other side of the counter so
I knew how important that
connection is for someone's
day. That recognition is
unique, and when we get it
right, it's magic," explains
Roberts.

Calling out someone's
name or knowing
their drink order
underscores that
personal connection
and it makes people
feel good.

—DAVINA PEREZ

Laolu's relationship with coffee growing up in Nigeria initially felt a world away from his experience of it after moving to the United States. "My memories from childhood are of my father drinking instant coffee, which is really common in Nigeria," he says. "It's hard to find good espresso and milk in Nigeria so lattes were a luxury, one that it took me moving to Brooklyn to be able to appreciate." But when considering how to bring the story of coffee's human connection to life, Laolu thought of his homes, both old and new. "Coffee goes beyond borders, reaching and connecting people." And he aimed with his work to express both coffee's vast global footprint and its ability to link us all. "In my art, the variegated coffee beans signify the different origins, roasts, and varietals and the range of colors symbolize the diversity of the ethically sourced beans from farmers all over the world," Laolu explains.

SEEING A PATTERN

Laolu's creative motto
and frequent hashtag—
"Everything is my
canvas"—couldn't be
more fitting for an artist
who thinks far beyond
traditional conceptual
borders. While there are
few backdrops his work
hasn't graced, the most
intimate canvas he works
with is the skin. Laolu is
rarely without his white
marker, the key implement
for completing the face and
body paint ritual he calls
the "Sacred Art of the Ori,"
a reflection of his Yoruba
culture. He takes a singular
and considered approach
to each person he paints,
because the elaborate
technique serves as his
interpretation of their
spirit or essence. While
his lines and patterns are
highly complex and can
take countless hours for
him to render, there's a
deeper meaning behind
each stroke. "I'm always
telling a story," he says.
"I weave these stories
throughout my art, and the
patterns and lines connect
them together."

Laolu x Starbucks

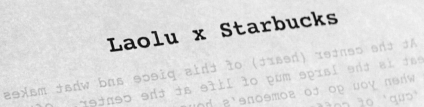

The colors within the art symbolize equality and ethically sourced beans from all over the world; the colors are both positive, showing responsibility and diversity. They also represent the diversity of the guests in each Starbucks location, as well as the farmers who grow the coffee, and the baristas who make it. Coffee goes beyond borders; coffee reaches and connects people.

—LAOLU

ARTIST

Q+A

Laolu

HOW WOULD YOU DESCRIBE YOUR ARTISTIC APPROACH?

My style of art is called "Afromysterics," meaning the mystery of the African thought pattern. I like to always weave stories throughout my work; my art is a visual narrative.

TELL US A BIT ABOUT THE STORY BEHIND THE ART YOU DREAMED UP FOR THE STARBUCKS PACKAGING?

The art is my telling of the story of Starbucks as *orisun*, a Yoruba word meaning "source," because for me Starbucks coffee is like a source of life.

WHAT ARE SOME OF THE KEY ELEMENTS IN YOUR PIECE THAT HELP TELL THAT STORY?

At the heart of the piece is the large mug of life with the rays stemming from it being the emotions of sharing that cup with someone. The different rays are also the lines of communication that connect us all. The music notes symbolize the different tasting "notes," and the masks represent the different people and communities that touch each bag of coffee, and the diversity of the Starbucks customers who will eventually enjoy the beverage. And there is the sun, without which we wouldn't be able to grow coffee or exist. Just like the sun, coffee is an infinite source of life and energy too.

WHAT DO YOU WANT YOUR ART TO EVOKE FOR THE CUSTOMER WHEN THEY SEE IT ON THE SHELVES?

I want them to feel happy and joyful and to feel connected and like family!

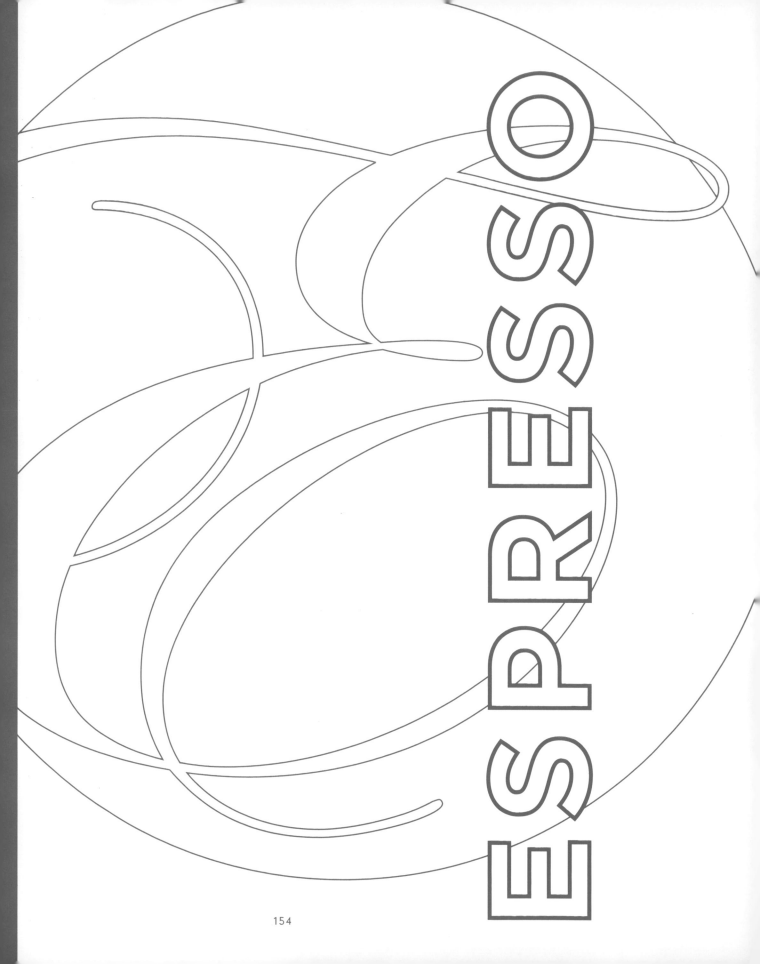

ESPRESSO

....

ESPRESSO ROAST

After experimentation with different blends and roasts, Starbucks®
Espresso Roast was first served in 1975, and has been the signature
espresso ever since. This bold blend with a hint of caramelly sweetness
perfectly complements steamed milk.

FLAVOR NOTES
Rich and caramel-like

GROWING REGION
Multi-region

BODY
Full

ACIDITY
Medium

PROCESSING
Washed, semi-washed

FOOD PAIRINGS
Brownies, chocolate croissants

BLONDE   MEDIUM   DARK

AT HOME

○

RECIPES

BREWING ESSENTIALS

Making a great cup of coffee at home doesn't have to be hard. The key is following a few simple brewing principles and understanding four fundamental elements of coffee making: water, grind, proportion, and freshness.

WATER

The bedrock for any coffee beverage is the water it starts with; if the water doesn't taste great, neither will the finished cup. A base of fresh, filtered water (which Starbucks has in all its stores) is key and so is the temperature: 195F°–205F° is the sweet spot at which a coffee's flavor can be properly extracted.

GRIND

An improper grind can result in unpleasant flavors in your cup. Too fine a grind can take the taste to a bitter place, while a grind that is too coarse may zap the coffee of its oomph, and give it a watery taste. For every brew method, there's a complementary grind, meant to extract the best and maximum flavor from the bean: coarse for a coffee press, medium for a drip, fine for a cone filter, and extra-fine for espresso.

PROPORTION

This is all about finding the ideal ratio of coffee to water so flavor can shine through. If you have too much coffee, it can result in a sour taste from under-extraction; too little coffee, and it can veer bitter. At Starbucks, the recommended ratio is two tablespoons of coffee for every six ounces of water.

FRESHNESS

Coffee actually shares more in common with fresh produce than with the contents of your pantry. Because light, heat, moisture, and oxygen can affect its freshness, and, in turn, its flavor, the clock starts on its expiration from the moment you open the bag. A few rules of thumb to keep your coffee at its best:

STORAGE It may seem counterintuitive but storing coffee in the refrigerator or freezer can expose it to moisture; instead, keep it in an airtight container at room temperature.

TIME A bag of whole beans will stay fresh longer than one that's been ground (grinding should happen right before brewing), but ideally it should still be consumed within a week of opening.

HEAT A coffee's flavor is delicate so letting it linger too long on a heat source will affect that. Never leave it on a burner or the heated surface of a drip coffee machine for more than twenty minutes. Best to transfer to a thermal carafe where it will retain its flavor integrity for about half an hour.

ICED CINNAMON COFFEE

···

SERVES 1

1-1/2 cups ice

10 oz. diluted unsweetened cold brew concentrate
(see page 169 for cold brew recipe) or 5 oz. double-strength
coffee (try Starbucks® Pike Place® Roast or Starbucks®
Cold Brew pitcher packs), shaken with additional ice

1 tablespoon sweetened condensed milk

Pinch of ground cinnamon

WITH COLD BREW Fill a tall glass with the ice and pour coffee over.
Add sweetened condensed milk and a pinch of cinnamon. Stir until well
mixed and enjoy.

WITH DOUBLE-STRENGTH COFFEE Fill a cocktail shaker with ice.
Add double-strength coffee, sweetened condensed milk, and cinnamon.
Shake until coffee is cooled and ingredients are well mixed. Pour into
a tall glass filled with ice and enjoy.

COLD BREW MILKSHAKE

· ·

SERVES 1

1/2 cup Starbucks® diluted cold brew concentrate
(see page 169 for recipe)

2 large scoops vanilla ice cream

2 tablespoons semisweet chocolate chips

Add all ingredients to a blender. Blend to taste, then pour into a tall glass.
Serve immediately.

IRISH COFFEE

· ·

SERVES 1

1 tablespoon brown sugar

1 cup hot brewed Starbucks® Caffè Verona® coffee

1-1/2 oz. Irish whiskey

Whipped cream

In a heat-safe glass or a mug, add brown sugar and pour coffee over. Stir until dissolved. Add whiskey. Garnish with whipped cream.

COFFEE NEGRONI

....

1 cup ice

1/2 oz. gin

1 oz. sweet vermouth

1 oz. Campari

2 oz. cooled iced coffee or diluted cold-brewed coffee
(try Starbucks® Espresso Roast, either iced or prepared
according to cold brew recipe on page 169)

1-1/2 oz. club soda

Wide orange peel or slice

In a tall glass, combine ice, gin, vermouth, and Campari. Stir to combine
and chill. Top with coffee and club soda. Garnish with orange peel or slice
and serve.

Coffee Negroni

Cold Brew Old Fashioned

COLD BREW OLD FASHIONED

SERVES 1

2 tablespoons orange syrup (see recipe on page 169)

4 dashes aromatic bitters

Ice

6 oz. cold brew concentrate (see recipe on page 169)

Brandied cherries (store-bought or homemade)

Orange peel

Combine 2 tablespoons orange syrup and bitters in a glass and stir. Add ice, then top with 6 oz. cold brew concentrate. Run inside of orange peel around the rim of the glass, twist peel, and add to drink along with a cherry. Stir again then serve.

FOR COLD BREW CONCENTRATE
(YIELDS APPROXIMATELY TEN 6 OZ. SERVINGS)

1 large Mason jar or pitcher with lid

1 piece of cheesecloth, for filter

1/4 lb. coffee, coarsely ground (Guatemala Antigua coffee
or Starbucks® Cold Brew pitcher packs are recommended)

1/2 gallon filtered water

Place ground coffee in a piece of cheesecloth and tie closed with string or a
strip of cheese cloth (similar to a sachet). Place the sachet of coffee in jar or
pitcher, and pour filtered water over sachet to saturate the coffee grounds.
Put lid on pitcher or jar and steep at room temperature for 12 hours (or up to
24 hours in refrigerator). Store in an airtight jar in refrigerator for up
to 5 days.

When ready to serve, dilute cold brew concentrate by adding 1 oz. water for
every 1 oz. of cold brew. Serve over ice and enjoy.

FOR ORANGE SYRUP
(YIELDS APPROXIMATELY 16 OZ.)

1 cup demerara or raw sugar

1 cup water

Peel from one orange

Combine all ingredients in a saucepan over medium heat and cook until
sugar dissolves and mixture just comes to a boil. Remove from heat and
cool completely. Remove orange peels and pour into a glass jar with a lid
or other storage container. Cover and store at room temperature.

SHAKERATO

....

1/2 cup milk of your choice (for a richer sweet cream
use a combination of whole milk and half and half)

1 tablespoon simple syrup for sweet cream,
plus 1/2 tablespoon for shaking

2 shots espresso

To make sweet cream, in a glass or small bowl, combine milk and
1 tablespoon simple syrup. Stir until well mixed and set aside. Add
espresso, ice, and remaining 1/2 tablespoon of simple syrup to
a cocktail shaker. Shake, pour into a glass, top with sweet cream
to taste, and enjoy.

COLD BREW HORCHATA

· ·

1/4 cup of diluted cold brew (see page 169),
using Starbucks® Caffè Verona coffee

1/4 cup cold filtered water

1/2 cup horchata (store bought or homemade)

Cinnamon for garnish

Pour diluted cold brew into a cocktail shaker. Add horchata and a
scoop of ice and shake for 10 seconds. Pour into a tall glass and top
with a sprinkle of cinnamon.

SPRONIC

Ice

4–6 oz. tonic water

3 dashes aromatic bitters

2 shots of espresso (Espresso Roast or Sumatra coffee)

Lemon wedge for garnish

Fill a glass with ice, then add tonic water until halfway full. Add aromatic bitters. In a cocktail shaker, shake espresso shots with more ice, then strain into glass with tonic water. Garnish with lemon wedge.

ICED COFFEE WITH ORANGE TWIST

SERVES 1

8 tablespoons coffee (try Pike Place® Roast or other Latin American or African coffees), ground for a paper pour-over filter (about the coarseness of granulated sugar)

12 oz. hot water (just off the boil), plus more for rinsing

2 cups of ice, plus 4–5 large ice cubes

Orange peel for garnish

FOR ICED COFFEE Briefly rinse a paper filter with hot water and discard rinse water. Add grounds to the filter, then fill halfway with hot water to saturate the grounds, then pause 10 seconds to let coffee bloom. (The coffee will bubble as it releases gases.) Slowly add the rest of the hot water in small steady circles to cover all of the grounds. When brewing has slowed to a drip, pour coffee over two cups of ice in a large jar or pitcher to dilute.

FOR DRINK Place 4–5 large ice cubes into a glass. Add desired amount of cold coffee. Using a vegetable peeler, peel a strip of orange peel (try to get as little pith as possible). Squeeze peel over coffee and ice and drop into the glass.

*Starbucks would like to thank the following
individuals and groups for their contributions
to the Coffee Stories program:*

Andy Adams
Peter Ahlberg
Sergio Alvarez
Brad Anderson
Beth Baggaley
Tania Barrett
Lara Behnert
Andres Berron
Calvin Blanchette
Colleen Brown
Wade Campbell
Anthony Carroll
David Carter
Ricardo Cavolo
Christine Chiarottino
Alisa Cohen
Doug Cohen
Leon Cortez
Joe Cunningham
Josie Daniels
Hansel Doan
Tristan Eaton
Mark Edwards
Marc-Kwesi Farrell
Jeffrey Fields
Sharon Frajlich
Ruby Francisco
Leanne Fremar
Mike Fuller
Geri Gale
Elizabeth Ghaly
Rebekah Gruenig
Carole Guizzetti
Levke Haas
Kent Hatcher
Brian Hayes
Sara Hendrickson
Julian Hom
Morgan Ione Yeager
Erik Inloes
Kyle Iskra
Kayleigh Junk
Divya Kakkad
Emily Kersch
Adele Kudish
Ann-Marie Kurtz
Caitlin Leffel
Destiny Linayao
Andrew Linnemann
Tovan Marhennata
Surip Mawardi
Mary Mayorquin

Donald McKinlay
Michael Mendonsa
Steve Murray
Harper McConnell
Lauren Nimmons
Hohan Nguyen
Melissa O'Hearn
Katie Rogantelli
Davina Perez
Sandor Petiet
Jen Picken
Erin Poulter
Jen Quotson
Ryan Rimsnider
Sandy Roberts
Adrienne Roesler
Brian Romine
Rich Ronald
Jennifer Ropell
Matthew Rossi
Rana Saab
Michael Schwarz
Laolu Senbanjo
Jeremy Sirbu
Elizabeth Smith
Sandy Stark
Anne Stevens
Fernando Stewart
Austin Tott
Katey Truhn
Jessie Unterhalter
Fiorella Valdesolo
Maggie Van Ness
Stephanie Vandenack
Anasazi Wade
Jake Walters
Tim Washington
Briar Waterman
Dave Wickberg
Jeff Wilkson
Drew Wilson
Amanda Wygal
Jake Yeagley
Pip Zebrowan
Sheryl Zeunert

The partners at the
9th & Broadway store, New York

The partners at the
11 Penn store, New York

2018 2019 2020 2021 / 10 9 8 7 6 5 4 3 2 1

Pike Place is a registered trademark of
The Pike Place Market PDA, used under license.

Designed by AHL&CO / Peter J. Ahlberg
Principal Photography by Morgan Ione Yeager
Text by Fiorella Valdesolo
Editor & Project Manager: Caitlin Leffel
Copy Editors: Elizabeth Smith, Adele Kudish
Retouching: Kyle Iskra

Additional photography on pages 44, 166, and 167
by Starbucks

Production by Lifeguard Press

Printed in China